Security Token Offerings for Beginners

D1279328

The Ultimate Guide to Security Tokens, Security Token Offerings and Tokenized Securities

© **Copyright 2018 - All rights reserved.**

Table of Contents

Introduction

2017 and 2018 were crucial years for the world of the blockchain and cryptocurrencies. In December 2017, the price of Bitcoin shot way over what anyone expected, almost surpassing its threshold of $20,000 in value and, altogether, an investment of around $6 billion was raised by ICOs.

Understandably so, excitement was rising high at these results, but the highs could not be sustained, not when all the hacks and scams, the sudden collapse, albeit temporary, of Bitcoin and silly errors from investors who hadn't a clue what they were doing were added into the mix. The market was hit hard, and the knock-on effect hit all crypto-enthusiasts who could only sit, white-faced, as they saw their investments appearing to crumble before their very eyes. It comes down to this – the one thing that attracted investors to the ICO market was the lack of regulation and controls and that has also proven to be one of the biggest weaknesses too.

The boom-times for the ICOs are gone. Yes, the best of the ICO projects will thrive and new ones will continue to emerge, albeit slower than they have done but 2018 was the start of something new – security token offerings – now seen in many countries as the safest and more reasonable response to the ICOs.

To start with, having the word "security" in the name ensures that the philosophy is easy to understand – any security token must be backed by tangible assets, such as corporate earnings for example. An STO also requires a license approved by the financial regulatory bodies of the country they exist in and that means they are regulated. STOS function as company share offerings, exploiting only the advantages of security tokens being used as digital resources and any tangible asset can be 'tokenized' and that includes real estate, or it can be used for supporting a security token.

Security tokens may also be used as a way of accelerating venture capital democratization. With the blockchain and the smart contracts, we saw an introduction to efficient ways of raising capital without needing an intermediary and this introduction also serves as the basis for security tokens to be created. As a fundraising vehicle, the tokens give a company the option of raising capital without the need to involve stock exchanges, investment banks, or any other financial middleman and this has been demonstrated very well by Securitize, Harbor and Polymath, along with other token businesses.

Given the fact that security tokens are regulated, and legal control is guaranteed by the regulatory body, investors no longer need to worry about whether a project is credible before they invest in it. All they need to worry about is whether the company will be financially successful, just like in the old days with stocks and that will make them more prone to risking their money. With capital much easier to access, we will see more and more companies on the rise and more and more of the unstable one's collapse. The STO will be a contributory factor in a meritocratic, unstable scenario; a scenario in which even venture capitalists can invest and get out quicker than they could before.

Blockchain technology and the technology behind the distributed ledger already allow for non-liquid assets to be tokenized, such as fine arts, real estate, and other categories of asset that were once reserved only for those at the top of the money scale. With a security token, a person can own a fraction of real estate that would otherwise cost millions, giving everyone the chance to get a piece of the action You could say that this is much the same as having shares in a REIT – a real-estate investment fund but security tokens offer a great deal more in the way of flexibility to investors of all shapes and sizes and they are not the only ones to take advantage of it.

Ready to learn more about security tokens and STOs? Want a bite of the cherry? Then dive in and learn.

Chapter 1: What is a Security Token?

Security tokens are set to be the next big thing on the blockchain revolution, following cryptocurrencies like Bitcoin, smart contracts from the likes of Ethereum, and utility tokens. If you had asked about these tokens a couple of years ago, all you would have got would be blank stares. They didn't exist before last year but now, everywhere you look, it's security tokens all the way. So, what are these security tokens?

Before you can understand that, you need to have at least a basic understanding of securities. A security is a financial asset that is tradable, like notes, debentures, bonds, options, warrants, stocks and shares. Let's use stocks and shares as an example; when you purchase them you are purchasing a part of or a share in a company without actually having possession of it.

This method is used by the government and companies to raise money from investors via the capital markets. The investors purchase on the promise that they will get a return on their investment in the form of interest shares, dividends, or a share of the profit in some way or another.

When all of this is done using a cryptographic token, it becomes known as a security token.

Putting it in more basic terms, a security token is a cryptographic token that pays out share profits, dividends, interest or investments in other assets or tokens that will generate some kind of profit for the holder. This takes care of liquidity, something that proved to be a huge problem with the paper-backed assets of old, like bonds, real estate or shares.

With a cryptographic representation, liquidity is no longer an issue.

Just imagine, dividends paid on a set date provided a specific condition is met using a smart contract. No hassle, no delays.

All of this can both automate and speed up the process because now you are dealing with security that is programmable. And this can do everything traditional security can do and a whole lot more besides.

Plus there is a high demand for this kind of security token because they are regulated by the relevant jurisdiction. In the US, for example, the Howey Test is used for determining if a crypto is, in fact, a security token or not. The Howey Test was devised by the Supreme Court as a way of determining whether a transaction could be qualified as an investment contract. If yes, then the Securities Act 1933 and the Securities Exchange Act 1934 dictate that the transaction is considered to be a security and that makes them subject to registration and disclosure requirements.

A transaction is considered to be a security when these four elements are in existence:

- The transaction involves a financial (monetary) investment;

- The transaction exists in a common enterprise;

- The transaction offers the expectation of a profit;

- The transaction is derived from the efforts of other people

Why the Market is Bullish about Security Tokens

The obvious reason for a bullish market is that the use cases for security tokens are pretty much unlimited. Right now, it is new territory, largely unexplored but the big banking firms and the major institutional investors are all placing high bets on the prospects of success.

Another reason is that it finally brings in the regulation the market needs for cryptographic tokens. A result of this is that projects will garner a good deal more investor support and trust. In turn, this brings liquidity, a cost-effective, fast and secure trading platform, and far more automation to the market, minimizing or removing altogether entire back offices.

Last and perhaps more important, more companies are looking for a way to use the blockchain technology and smart contracts in their daily business and security tokens give them an easy and secure way to do just that.

A brand-new infrastructure would also be required because the old model is just too out of date. For security tokens, we would need:

- Exchanges and marketplaces

- Security Token Offerings (STOs)

- Custodians

- Wallets

- And so on

Another reason for a bullish market is that there is just so much opportunity to be taken advantage of. Some SEC-regulated tokens are already beginning development of the infrastructure that will allow real-world assets to be securitized, including Polymath, tZero and Open Finance Network.

Leading us onto the next chapter, there is one thing you need to be aware of – some security tokens will attempt to act like a utility token and these are not SEC-regulated. To understand the differences between security and utility tokens, head on to chapter 2.

Chapter 2: Security Tokens vs. Utility Tokens

Now that the SEC (Securities and Exchange Commission) are cracking down on ICOs, it's easy to believe that the days of the ICO are numbered. That may not be the case. Sure, the SEC is gaining ground and going after ICOs and token sales that fail to register or make false claims and statements in their marketing. Fraudulent token sales should be forbidden. But there is also signs to the opposite. Every week there are ICOs coming out of the woodwork that are still allowed by governments across the world and the SEC. This naturally raises the question: based on which criteria do these regulatory bodies come to a decision about whether or not a token sale should be allowed?

The answer lies in the categorization and classification of an ICO and the token being issued. Pay close attention, because the following two terms will be essential to your understanding of the rest of this book. Basically, tokens can fall into one of two categories of tokens:

- Utility tokens
- Security tokens

Security Tokens

These are cryptographic tokens that investors get issued with when they participate in an ICO or a token sale in exchange for cash. A security token is one that pays share profits, dividends, interest or provides some other value to the token holder.

The USA and some other countries prohibit these tokens and, in order to be allowed, the token must be SEC-compliant BEFORE the token sale or ICO. However, because the blockchain and ICOs have garnered so much interest in recent times some new founders and start-ups have begun ignoring that fact and many security tokens have been launched without the SEC even being aware of them.

This is why the US government launched a crackdown on unregulated tokens and ICOs to keep investors safe. The rules are simple – if the token is a security token it must abide but the SEC rules and it must pass the Howey Test.

The US and the SEC are not set against ICOs and tokens as a rule, only the unregulated ones.

Utility Tokens

Utility tokens are otherwise known as app tokens or coins and they are called utility tokens because they must have some kind of utility in a decentralized application being built or that an ICO has been raised for.

There are a few examples of these tokens already out, but one thing that investors need to know is that some projects will present as a utility token when they clearly are not one. And utility tokens are finite in supply; because of this, some teams will attempt to promote their token as an investment opportunity. Why? Quite simply, supply and demand. If something becomes very popular and demand is high, the price rises.

But the SEC has their eye on these so before you invest in any ICO or token you need to be aware of the utility or the economics behind it before you part with your money. Three of the pure utility tokens are:

- Ether
- Sia
- Filecoin

So, to sum up, the differences between a security and a utility token:

Security	Utility
Asset ownership	access to the utility or the protocols
Investors expect a profit	no guarantee of any profit
Regulated – KYC*	Unregulated

*KYC – Know Your Customer

Two more things to bear in mind – not all utility tokens are a good thing. In fact, investment in utility tokens is far riskier because it is highly dependent on the application that the app token is made for. And, with an ICO, if it presents as a utility but is actually a security token, and the SEC comes down on them, your investment money is going to be held up for some considerable time.

The message is clear – be very aware of what you are investing in. If in any doubt, step back and do some more research. In basic terms, if a token is a security token it must be SEC-compliant.

Chapter 3: The Advantages of a Security Token

In time, the traditional financial products we all know will become digital and placed onto a blockchain, providing extra security and lower fees. With security tokens, investors will benefit in many ways, as will the issuers. Even the regulators will gain some benefit so let's take a look at just what advantages a security token has:

Compliance

And more of it. Right now, SEC and other word regulators are not too happy about security tokens, but that will change. Regulators are busy trying to manage numerous crypto projects, trying to work how existing laws can be applied and whether they are securities or otherwise.

At the moment, what the authorities are trying to deal with is something akin to the Wild West, but in time it will become much easier. With security tokens regulators will be able to apply more control, more compliance instead of less. Regulators today tend to be reactive rather than proactive – too much time and money is spent on finding the rule breakers, followed by years and years of numerous trials and prosecutions and not all of them will be successful.

Security tokens can shake things up in this area, placing the regulators firmly back in control and allowing them to be proactive in their governance. Smart contracts and the blockchain technology make it entirely possible for law and ownership to be written to a token and that means the token will be able to execute itself, regulate itself and even govern itself. For example, tokens may be programmed to determine who can and can't buy or sell it and that leads to holders of the tokens being restricted in who they can trade to – if the receiver hasn't passed the verification, they can't reassure the issuer that only authorized investors will hold it – that means, no trade.

There could also be a restriction on the transfer of tokens. For example, regulation D in the SEC rules states that investors cannot transfer or sell their ownership for a period of 12 months after the purchase, and that is a minimum. This regulation could be programmed directly to the token, ensuring that no trade or transfer can take place until that time period has passed.

If all that wasn't enough, a complete audit trail along with all the data right from when the token was created, and all the compliance processes are on the blockchain – a transparent ledger that anyone can see. As such, regulators could cut their compliance costs significantly, saving not only money but resources and energy too and their annual $1.6 billion budget will go a lot further.

New Investors

As a result of the benefits for regulators, eventually, the authorities will come to accept security tokens, supporting their implementation. This, in turn, will lead to massive opportunities for token issuers, providing them access to a global capital pool and the ability to reach out to a potentially huge base of investors.

When the time comes that security tokens may be globally traded, in theory, anyone who has an internet connection and who is within the regulatory limits will be able to access them and that will result in capital market access being democratized, not just for companies, but for any investor.

The framework that regulates the security tokens is one more reason why the community will be able to invest without having to worry about fraud and scams – this is what happened with many who invested in ICOs. With security tokens, all an investor needs to concern themselves with is whether the issuer is viable in an economic sense.

With large assets being fractionalized, even more investors will be able to get a foot in the door of a market that would normally only be open to those with serious money. They will be able to own a fraction of a stock, a tiny piece of real estate or a smidgeon of fine art; this may well upset the applecart as far as those investors with the money to buy the entire lot or who are prepared to invest for a much longer term, but it gives the ordinary investor on the street an 'in' as it were.

Liquidity

That fractional ownership leads to much lower minimum investments and that will increase liquidity. As more people step in and purchase a small stake, more and more assets once deemed to be illiquid will suddenly become more liquid on the blockchain. For example, a person who owns a very expensive piece of real estate can only turn into cash if there is someone willing to pay the entire asking price. With security tokens, that real estate will suddenly become liquid as more people can purchase a share in it rather than the entire thing.

The Mayfair Gallery is one of the best-known and earliest examples of art tokenization. They have placed their whole collection of fine art onto the blockchain including a piece by Andy Warhol that was valued at over $5 million. Many real estate companies are attempting to use the blockchain technology to give them a wider customer base by tokenizing some properties.

And perhaps the largest point in its favor is that the world of security tokens is not governed by opening hours, or by weekends. Instead, the market is open 24/7, 365 days a year the whole world over, thus pushing liquidity to heights never seen before int eh markets.

Efficient and Scalable

Both smart contracts and blockchain technology can potentially take the place of many of the current financial practices that are simply too costly and inefficient. By tokenizing securities, we have the potential to:

- Cut costs by eliminating some of the back offices still required by banks
- Simplify the processes for auditing and accounting
- Automate AML and KYC processes – there won't be a need for a back office to vet all investors
- Reduce the paperwork and the complexity of security management – signature collection, wiring funds, mailing checks, etc.
- Reduce issuance fees by taking the middleman out the investment equation
- Decrease reliability on lawyers over the long term by using smart contracts
- Enable settlements in real-time between buyers and sellers on the secondary market, thus reducing the risks associated with the settlement
- Use more smart contracts to enable automation through software of the service provider function
- Automate dividend pay-outs
- Enable proxy voting

- Provide better valuations of assets because the market will be freer and far more

Transparency

With the blockchain, we have a uniform method to track and verify data and also for preventing the data from being tampered with because it is immutable, i.e., it cannot be changed. With all this in place, the blockchain is the ideal infrastructure to document security ownership in a way that is completely transparent. This results in easier reporting, auditing and a better way of preventing fraud, not to mention issues with mispricing, corruption and manipulation.

Low Entry Barrier

With a traditional IPO, it takes time to float on an Alternative Investment Market or on the stock exchange and it is a tough process that only large companies who want to target several million dollars can make use of. It takes middlemen – a lot of them, including exchanges, brokers and so on – and it costs a small fortune.

By contrast one of the biggest advantages to security token offerings is that any asset can be tokenized in a fairly easy way for online trading. What this means is that the smaller businesses and the new start-ups can easily raise the capital they need without the addition of fees.

Over time, legal documentation is becoming more and more standard and more open source token protocols are appearing and this will result in the cost associated with running an STO coming down. As this happens, the entry barrier will be lowered even further, and more businesses can raise the money they need.

More Global Investors

Because standards for tokens tend to be uniform across regions, it is much easier for global investors to buy and trade tokens. Security tokens are far more liquid than a traditional private share because they are less costly, and time consume to trade with.

As a result, security token offering appeal to a different kind of profile than the AIM or stock markets do. Often, contributions are attracted from global investors who want a great return with better liquidity, raising more money quickly and getting the word out about a business to a much wider audience.

Hard-Coded Compliance

Compliance is a little bit more involved with an STO than it is with an ICO, but it is still easier to hard-code it into the security using blockchain standards like that developed on Ethereum. KYC checks, for example, could be coded so only investors who are accredited can trade them. As standards get better, it should become almost impossible for security regulations to be violated.

It should be fairly obvious to anyone that the blockchain technology can provide massive opportunities for a more efficient and open securities marketplace. However, right now, there are few security tokens on offer for trading and there are still a lot of challenges to be faced:

- The conundrum of being decentralized, scalable, secure and friendly all at the same time must still be solved
- More education is needed along with lobbying and persuading the relevant authorities that this is a great opportunity that needs to be grasped right now
- And the connection between on and off-chain needs to be in working order so that physical assets can be

brought to the blockchain, along with both national and international laws.

Chapter 4: The Disadvantages of a Security Token

So, we can see that there are plenty of advantages to security tokens, but like everything, it follows that there will be some downsides. Not too many though which is good news and none of these disadvantages are insurmountable so watch this space.

Compliance is More Complex

As I said earlier, a security token must still come under the regulations for existing securities and this means that any company running an STO must comply with the regulations that apply if they were floating an IPO.

There is a small advantage to the STO – some of the compliance factors can be hard-coded into the smart contract and token which means that, after issuance, the token is inherently more tradable. However, there is still a risk in that the complexities of the regulations must cross multiple jurisdictions so getting it right the first time is incredibly important.

That means you need to have a team with experience and with a background in business together with experts from the relevant fields, dependent, of course, on the assets being tokenized. With an ICO, creating value relies heavily on the technology whereas, with a security token, the value is derived from the business operations and that's why things need to be very tight indeed.

Legal expertise will also be required to cover each and every region that the tokens are being sold in, to make sure that the regional securities regulations are complied with. However, the good news is, there are specialist platforms, like Tokeny, for STOs that often provide this for you.

Platform Required

Where a traditional security relies on brokers and exchanges dotted around the world, the security token is somewhat different. You can't just ring your NOMAD or broker and ask them to create these tokens for you. An STO requires that your tokens are created by you along with the platform required to manage sales of the tokens. Get this bit wrong and the legal and financial ramifications don't bear thinking about.

Security tokens require a suitable platform that is entirely secure and creating one is nothing short of complex. That means a middleman is required to help manage both the platform and the tokens and this won't be free. However, there is one advantage to having a trusted partner – you don't need to deal with any of the complex frameworks and can concentrate on the creation of value.

The Market is Young

The very first security token offering was born less than two years ago and that makes this one of the newest spaces. Nothing has really been given an extensive test over the long-term and that means the risks for both the investor and the business are that much higher.

As a result, legal precedent is short in supply and there is nothing to say that the regulators won't turn back on their decisions at a moment's notice. For example, let's assume that a crooked trader managed to find a method of cheating at a sale. This could result in the securities commissions bringing in brand new regulations that could put your STO in jeopardy and could limit token liquidity.

Right now, there are no indications that new laws are going to be enacted so, for now, everything is looking good.

Chapter 5: Security Token Offerings, ICOs and IPOs

An STO is a security token offering, one of the newest and most legitimate methods of funding the latest blockchain innovations. Any STO must be licensed by the SEC or other relevant regulatory body and, in basic terms, it all comes down to traditional assets being tokenized into security tokens.

How They Work

A security token provides an investor with a way of purchasing a fraction of whatever the token is representing – real, estate, fine art, derivatives, etc., - in a digital format. With an STO we get far more liquidity, traceability and accessibility and because they are licensed, i.e., compliant with regulations, they are also protected against fraud.

On top of that, if a company were to fail, there would be a lot more accountability, whether they fail to report as per the rules or they just fail in general. All of this makes security tokens much more viable and plausible, leading to more investors and more money flowing in.

Security tokens are used for raising capital for an existing company or for a startup. This is logical given the concept behind an IPO or an ICO. In the US alone, over half a million companies are established on a yearly basis. And the likes of Silicon Valley, Wall Street and all the venture capitalists there are cannot possibly provide enough capital for them all. As a result, the STOs that are legally compliant and regulated provide another source for these companies to raise their capital. Although ICOs and STOs raised over $5.5 billion in

2017, in the same year in the US alone, IPOs raised over $36 billion.

Security tokens also work in helping to tokenize or securitize real-world assets already in existence. The tokenization process, also called crypto-fractionalization, of these assets is representative of yet another opportunity and a huge advantage for the security tokens. Global equity assets are valued in the region of $70 trillion, with real estate assets trouncing that at $230 trillion - $32 trillion for commercial, $180 trillion for residential and the rest in agricultural. All of these are potential security token seeds, formulating a brand new and emerging market.

The vast amounts of paperwork required for traditional security trading will eventually be replaced with security token adoption and these tokens will reduce the cost of administering the financial systems of today. The estimated world savings are around $6 billion yearly, just in paper systems, if mass adoption of the tokens is taken up across the equity markets.

The Difference between STOs, ICOs, and IPOs

We'll start with the ICO, the Initial Coin Offering. With an ICO, the company does not need to see any equity and tokens may be purchased for use, great for both companies. With a utility token, you have access to the services or products of the specific company, but you won't be investing in the actual company and, as a token user you are actually not entitled to a single thing. To be honest, the value is nil until the company in question delivers on their promise and that might take forever, if at all. In short, all you're purchasing is hope.

Most of the ICOs are way behind their schedule or they have already gone and if they take your money with them, well there's nothing you can do about it. So that begs the question, is this the right time for an alternative, or should we be concentrating on fixing the existing mess?

The answer to that question lies in another question – why are STOs being considered as a viable alternative?

The STO is legitimate and stable, two things that many ICOs simply aren't. Security tokens are tied to a real security, which in turn is representative of a tokenized asset. Asset classes are worth an eye-watering amount of money and this can potentially provide the crypto market with a huge boost.

Because of the uncertainty that surrounds future regulation, many ICOs are heading for a world of legal hurt at some time or another. STOs will meet the compliance regulations right from the start.

It is a huge deal having no threat of interference from governments while an assurance that a token is a utility token is no comfort whatsoever. With security tokens that fully meet the regulatory rules, the risks are removed.

We already know that there have been multiple fraud cases, illegal activities and scams that surround ICOs and registration with the SEC, or another relevant regulatory body, reduces that risk significantly – less risk equals more investor confidence.

The Other Side of the Coin

There are downsides, of course, not least the amount of complexity and paperwork that come with STOs. The ICO hasn't brought too much of that kind of trouble just yet. In fact, with an ICO, it has been a little too easy to raise somewhat stupid amounts of money and it's clear to see why teams issue ICOs. However, it is also clear that this kind of money-raising method is starting to die out with investors beginning to see that there is little sense in the token economics.

One issue that has come to light with STOs is that some will not allow retail investors to join a sale. When a security hits a regulated exchange, algorithmic trading takes care of most of the trades, bringing about centralizations. ICO access was more open to accredited investors but not exclusively.

Yet another issue is that token demand is based highly on current and future value, rather like a tool for speculation. And for as long as tokens are listed on exchanges this will continue to happen.

Theoretically, STOs bright many benefits but we still need time to see how they will work in reality.

At a glance:

STOs	ICOs
Fraud protection set up	easy to
Based on real-world assets accessible	highly
Fully regulated and compliant investor has all of the risks	the
Incorporation into the market for greater securities speculative, promise-based	
No room for retail investors somewhat dubious in legal terms	
Loads of legal paperwork	

IPOs

There is some confusion over the difference between an IPO and an STO. A security token offering is a public offering that is regulated, but it is very new. The IPO, or Initial Public Offering, has been around for years – I bet you didn't know that the very first one was in 1602, well over 400 years ago!

Today, there are insiders who think that the STO is about to cause huge disruption to the IPO market. However, such statements are easy to throw about and easy to believe so research is imperative so you can make your own mind up. Yes, there is a good chance that the STO will take over from the IPO but not, perhaps, as quickly as some would expect. STOs and their tokens are regulated which means they have the services and the infrastructures needed for proper market functioning. This makes them licensed activities and both compliance and licensing take time and money to achieve. As such, there is a bigger barrier of entry compared to the IPO and that makes them slower than an IPO, despite offering the quality and certainty that is missing from ICO markets.

Because the IPO has been around a lot longer, it tends to be the go-to method for established companies to raise money. An established company is one that already has a working product or service, and enough viable results or growth metrics. At the end of the day, most IPOs are done by companies that require significant capital to keep their growth going and these are just the kind of companies that the STOs need in order to attract the capital and the investors.

If there is no quality in the available companies, there will be no investors for the STOs, so it is unlikely, right now, that the STO will take the place of the IPO, which is already a proven method for raising money. Certainty is one of the most important factors, especially when there is significant money at risk. Imagine a CFO. First, he pushes for an STO and it fails. The likely outcome is his or her job is gone. Now images that they push for an IPO and that fails. They will likely keep their job because they only did what was expected of them.

Most people are inherently averse to risk so psychological factors are always an important consideration when it comes to fast security token adoption. In time, as STOs push on and we see more success, this will cease to be an issue.

At the current time, the traditional stock market has plenty of liquidity whereas the exchanges for the security tokens are only just starting and it isn't clear whether they can produce fantastic products and sufficient liquidity to provide a viable token market. And we can't tell when it will happen either.

It is expected that there will be plenty of options, much the same way as we have those options with traditional stock exchanges. And some of the traditional exchanges are branching out into security tokens. For example, OKEX, Binance, and other crypto platforms are jointly working with the Malta Stock Exchange to launch platforms to trade security tokens on and you will find several others like this across the world, including the London Stock Exchange, tZero, Templum, Open Finance, and the Australian Securities Exchange. We saw cryptocurrencies reaching dizzy heights that nobody ever thought possible – that will happen with the security token exchanges; we just don't know when and, for now, the IPO will remain as the fundraising method of choice for many companies.

Chapter 6: Finding the Best STO

So, where do you find a decent STO to potentially invest in? Below is a list of some of the websites that offer information on current security or equity token offerings, but a word of warning before you continue reading – this is purely for informational purposes and I am NOT giving you any investment advice. Do all your own research before you invest money, be very careful, and please never invest any more than you can comfortably afford to lose.

Before we go into the list, my research has kicked up that the only companies that have so far received any significant investor attention and demand are the crypto asset infrastructure companies like tXero, tokenized real estates, like St Regis Aspen Resort and blockchain fund companies, like Science Blockchain and Blockchain Capital. However, there are now several more types of offering looking set to become available, like traditional companies who want their equity tokenized. However, there are a few factors that are limiting demand right now, including:

- STOs are far too new for there to be any real documented cases on non-blockchain company success
- The infrastructure is very young and that causes a certain amount of concern over when investors can expect to see liquidity
- Right now, understanding is quite low in many traditional equity companies on what an STO is and how they can get involved in one
- Predominant scrutiny because of the slowdown in ICO utility tokens.

As such, as far as non-crypto companies go right now, we are yet to see any real evidence of performance in terms of STO fundraising, but that situation can change in a heartbeat as the infrastructure is developed, but dependent on which way regulators go.

Websites to Check

icobench.com

The number one platform for ICO ratings provides an up to date list of all current ICOs and STOs.

stoanalytics.com

Lists all security tokens and STOs including real estate, investment fund, traditional company, etc.

token.security

Provides a full list of the top security token issuance companies along with those that provide advice and are involved in security token infrastructure design and development.

investinblockchain.com

Provides very detailed information about security token projects on the blockchain.

coinintelligence.com

This website is aimed more at discussing the security token exchanges that are expected to launch in 2019 as well as those already up and running.

stoscope.com

A very detailed website that provides information on current security token projects, STOs – current, due to expire and due to start – along with a list of STO services.

tokenmarket.net

Along with news about security tokens and STOS, this website also provides a handy calendar that lists all the STOs, when they open and close along with all those yet to be announced. It also offers you the option of subscribing to alerts so you never miss out on upcoming STOs.

coinsutra.com

Provides details on the current top five security token issuance platforms. This is kept updated so, as things start to change, you can expect to see this list updated.

stocheck.com

Another website offering a full list of STOs, including the sector they are in, plus details of public and private sales.

icomarks.com

ICOMarks provides an updated list of the STOs on offer right now, including details of presales, start and end dates of the offering and is always kept updated.

securities.io

As well as current news on the security token scene, this website also provides a list of companies that are currently raising funds or who have who already been fully funded.

No doubt there are more sources for security token listings, but these are the top ones that are always kept up to date with the latest information. To be honest, if you can't find it on one of these sites then it probably isn't really worth a look right now.

Chapter 7: Analyzing STO White Papers

The fast-rising interest in security token offerings has led to a growing demand for white paper writers and because they are similar to security offerings, an STO white paper has specific guidelines to follow to ensure it is legal. One of the best ways to analyze a white paper for an STO is to understand the way in which they are written.

Just like with conventional ICOs, an STO white paper is the most essential and cornerstone marketing document for any company conducting an STO; it deserves great attention as even small mistakes in the white paper can make a venture die before it even sees the light of day. Given that there are as of now no legally binding guidelines and standards that STO white papers have to follow (as opposed to securities prospectus for regular shares), it is even more important that a white paper conforms to language that is neither leading nor speculative.

When the ICOs arrived on the scene, we saw a number of fake writers who claimed to be experts; not surprising given that many ICOS claimed the same and many of the white papers cost little more than $100 to produce – seriously not worth the paper they were written on! The trick with a white paper is to learn to tell the difference between the real thing and a cheap fake and because STOs are regulated, the white papers tend to be tighter and, in a word, legal.

You could say that an STO is nothing more than an ICO with a consultation with a real-life lawyer before the token offering goes ahead. In fact, it's safe to say that, as far as legal compliance goes, it isn't a luxury; it is a requirement and failure to follow it can lead to dire consequences for all concerned.

So, without any further ado, let's look at how a white paper for an STO is made up so you can understand it and learn to analyze the information within.

STO White Paper Sections

All STO white papers must contain these six sections in order to ensure that the document is complete:

- **Legal Disclaimers**
- **Industry and Market Overview**
- **Technical Details of the Product**
- **Tokenomics and Details of the Token Offering**
- **Business Model**
- **Members of the Team and STO Advisors**

There is no set order for these sections, but the order listed above does tend to offer a more natural feel and lets anyone reading the paper follow the story in a cohesive manner.

Legal Disclaimers

These may also be called Forward-Looking Statements and are provided by a legal firm or agency once they have reviewed the entire white paper. The following should be included in the disclaimers:

- **Profit Expectation Clauses** – Because an STO allows for profit to be expected, product vetting must legally state what the profit expectation is, how that profit is to be delivered and what the risks are.

- **Allowed Countries** – because security tokens are similar in nature to equities and the fact that they are governed by laws that also govern equities, the STO will exclude at least one country from the STO if a specific country is allowed. For example, Under the US Patriot Act, US citizens are not allowed to make any investment in South Sudan, Libya and a couple of other notified countries. As such, an STO in which Libyan nationals may participate may not include Americans. This information must be listed in the white paper.

- **Token Ownership Rights and Benefits** – With an STO, the architecture of the token may be designed in such a way that voting rights, dividend rights and ownership of the asset that backs the token may be provided.

- **Token Sales Event Privacy Policy** – This is to tell the reader how data that is stored in an STO system is used. Since the new GDPR rules came into pay for European citizens, the privacy policy has become even more important and a white paper for an STO must have either the privacy policy or a link to it listed.

Industry and Market Overview

All STOs will either address the operations of at least one industry or they will disrupt them. The Industry Overview section is vital, but it is the one section that many ICO white papers left out. STOs will have a diverse range of investors and many will know nothing about the industry, how it works, what it's all about, etc. As such, this section provides a huge amount of information for the reader's benefit. It must include:

- **Industry History** – this should be a page that tells readers about the history of the specific industry, about previous developments and innovations, inventions and everything that has gotten the industry to where it is now. It must be a balanced overview and it must pinpoint the problem area that the STO wants to solve. For example, if the STO is aimed at solving supply chain management issues then the white paper must discuss the middlemen and the problems that slow the process down, writing off much of the value that has been created.

- **Stakeholder Constraints** – this should be one to two pages for each stakeholder. STOs are designed to address problems experienced by at least one stakeholder, usually more, having an effect on how the stakeholders currently function. The solution being proposed will include a learning curve and the stakeholders are unlikely to want this so it is crucial that the white paper discusses the problems that exist as a way of reminding stakeholders that there is a need for movement and innovation.

- **Emerging Trends** – two pages discussing other solutions aside from the STO that can solve the problem being addressed followed by a presentation on how and why the STO is the best solution.

- **Market Potential** – two pages that discuss the market potential of the STO. Charts, infographics, graphs, and so on, should be included to present data on the market size that already exists, the potential future size and how the STO will scale.

Technical Details of the Product

This is the longest part of the white paper and should contain the most information. If you look at a white paper and this section only has a couple of pages with limited information, it's a sure bet it hasn't been written properly and isn't worth a second look. However, just because it has the most information it doesn't follow that it will be reams of pages long (the technical architecture is the longest). It should, however, tie together the loose ends from the previous section and present the STO as the right solution in a natural way.

For example, if the STO white paper is offering a real-estate tokenization solution it must discuss the constraints that surround buyers, builders and regulating authorities. It should also discuss the way that the STO addresses those problems and should be divided down into sections:

- **Overview of the solution** – this should be a page detailing the product briefly. It is highly likely that the solution will be made up of multiple modules that each communicates with the others to become one unit. Let's assume that the company wants to create an exchange for cryptocurrencies. In this case, the section would have to contain the portfolio, wallet and a trading module (algorithmic), all connected at the backend. However, the section would also have to contain screenshots of how the user interface will look at the front-end. After all, this is how the exchange is going to be used by its clients. The solution section must have a short paragraph on each module along with a diagram showing how they connect.

- **Details of the Solution** – this should be between five and 10 pages long, dependent on how complex the STO solution is. It should not go over 10 pages and it must drive the point home that this solution is the only one out of all of them that will solve the problem/s. For example, if the STO is for a solar plant, the solution details must say how the tokens can be bought, how the solar plant will be built, how misuse will be prevented and must include front-end components details, such as a desktop or a mobile app.

Tokenomics and Token Offering

Let's briefly touch on the term "tokenomics" or "token economics". Too many companies and wannabe crypto-experts get this wrong. Token economics are NOT about how many tokens will be created and how they are distributed – this information is covered among the token offering in general.

The token economics section however lays out the incentives and rewards for the different stakeholders of the platform. It describes clearly why the tokenization of the underlying assets is meaningful. It is necessary to explain how each of the stakeholders are going to benefit from using the platform's native tokens instead of merely using other cryptocurrencies or FIAT currencies. Only if this section makes sense and goes into detail, then the value of the token can be maintained and increased over time.

Therefore: look out for a token economics section and read it multiple times to make sure it really makes sense. If it seems suspicious to you and there is no clear incentive or rewards for users and suppliers to use the token on the platform, then be warned! It may be time to move on to research STOs that make more sense!

Given that the token economics make sense, you should also look for the following information in the general token sale section:

- How many tokens will be created for sale and what happens if insufficient sales are made

- The initial price of a token

- How investors can buy and trade the tokens, including the percentage reserved for public sale

- Details of dividend distribution and token usage

- Risk factors

Ideally, the publishing company has put all of this information into a single two-column table, making it easy for you to review the essential token sale details.

Business Model

This section must describe the way in which the company creates value, delivers it and captures it in all relevant contexts. Business models are generally broken down into three sections:

- The process of creating the value; in the case of an STO, this would describe how the asset is being tokenized and why

- The process of selling the value; the tokens and the token offering details, including marketing and delivery

- How the customer pays and what they pay; an overview of pricing, the offering details, payment methods, etc.

In a nutshell, the business model is purely an exploration of the costings and expenditure against potential profit.

Members of the Team and STO Advisors

This section should introduce each person on the team, detailing their background and their experience, along with the role they play in the team and what their goal is. There are likely to be several team members and every one of them must be introduced here so that readers can get to know the team that runs their potential investment.

This isn't set in stone but, when you are analyzing an STO white paper to see if an STO is a viable product or not, there should be sufficient information to tell you what, why and how.

Chapter 8: STO Participation and Security Exchanges

Participating in STOs is much the same as participation in an ICO. Once the security token offering has been issued and selling period has been set, investors can purchase a number of tokens, which they can then later sell, or trade. The tokens would be representative of a tangible asset, some kind of profit, company shares and so on.

Right now, the only people who can participate in a private sale of security tokens are accredited investors. These investors must meet specified SEC requirements about their net income, annual income, and what type of institution is participating, i.e. trust, venture fund, etc.

Security Token Exchanges

The one thing that is needed, like the cryptocurrencies, is a security token exchange platform. In 2017, Gibraltar hit the headlines when the Gibraltar Stock Exchange owner, GSX Group Limited, made an announcement at the FinTech summit in Hong Kong – they were creating a brand new subsidiary called GBX – the Gibraltar Blockchain Exchange. This subsidiary had the goal of creating a "new standard of excellence," and this would be achieved by only letting listings that were high quality and fully vetted to be offered through their new global and regulated utility token marketplace.

At around the same time as GBX was announced, GSX Group Limited also confirmed that the Gibraltar Stock Exchange was going to undergo a revamp. The stock exchange, owned by GSX, would become the very first regulated exchange in the world for security token listings and trades. Although the news went very much under the radar at the time of the announcement, this was and remains a huge deal. The whitepaper that GSX published stated that they intended to be listing tokenized securities by the third quarter of 2018 and have security token trading enabled by the fourth quarter. This is yet to happen, but GSX is now officially approaching the GFSC (Gibraltar Financial Services Commission) seeking regulatory approval for listing and trading security tokens, expected to start in the first quarter of 2019. Obviously, GSX has not met the timeline they originally set out, but the point remains the same. For an exchange licensed in the EU to recognize security, tokens is a huge deal for the entire blockchain community and one that will continue to be watched very closely.

News aside, there are several projects that are well worth a look, mostly in the US, despite no small amount of uncertainty regarding the regulatory climate and we'll detail them here.

OpenFinance Network

One of the more interesting projects that have started taking shape in the US is OFN, the OpenFinance Network. OFN claims that they are the very first regulated platform for security tokens in the USA and here's all you need to know about them.

The OFN platform is three-fold – trading, clearing and settlement – for alternative assets, a combination of a matching system (centralized) with a P2P settling process (decentralized). The platform first went live in June of this year after several months of beta tests, carried out by partners and early investors. However, it only sort of went live and the administrators have now clarified that you can't actually trade yet; all you can do is register with the platform and complete the KYC process.

That said, even when it eventually does go live for trading, investors will only be able to trade with one token to start with – SpiCE VC, which is a VC fund that has been tokenized. The team behind OFN has said that, in time, they expect to see BCAP, or Blockchain Capital, which is another fund that has been tokenized, to use the platform for trading but no solid timelines have been set out just yet. There is no doubt that the OFN team is working hard on this and have, so far, made some important partnerships, including Republic and Polymath. And they have announced that they have a pipeline for token listing that contains more than 130 security tokens whose combined market cap is over $6 billion. Again, we have no solid indication of when we can start trading the tokens.

A few other important points to note – it is possible for a non-accredited investor to create an OFN account but, until either Reg A or Reg CF tokens are issued, they cannot trade. Reg A and Reg CF are two of the regulations that pertain to the raising of private capital, both introduced by JOBS Act 2015. Investors are also required to use MetaMask, which is a popular browser interface and wallet, but this doesn't offer anywhere near the security that investors want.

tZero

tZero is another of the projects that is coming out of the USA and this one has gotten itself a great deal more attention than OFN has and that is down to the fact that its parent, Overstock, is huge. However, not all of the headlines about tZero have been good news. Their STO couldn't have gotten off to a worse start when the SEC announced that they were investigating tZero. This was followed by a prominent law firm filing a class action lawsuit against Overstock and named officers of the company after securities were sold in violation of the federal securities laws.

All this aside though, the tZero platform definitely has the potential to be one of the biggest players in the trading of security tokens, mostly because it already has the operation capacity, access to the capital it needs and some very ambitious plans. Here's all you need to know.

tZero currently owns SpeedRoute LLC and PRO Securities LLC, both broker-dealers who are SEC-registered and members of FINRA. The tZero platform has four main areas – brokerage services, smart order routing, management systems for stick inventory and 24-hour trading. Right now, only traditional equities can be traded on the platform, but a system for trading security tokens is now being developed. tZero has a pretty impressive infrastructure too. At the time of writing, between 15 and 18 million traditional equity orders are processed every day and the company says it can easily handle more than 100 million every day.

In May of this year, tZero announced that they intended to collaborate with BOX Holdings to form an exchange that companies could list on and investors could trade, publicly, with security tokens. tZero is putting the money and the tech up while BOX is providing the people and the expertise in regulatory rules. Of course, the SEC has to approve this deal and that is not guaranteed but, should they get the go-ahead, the collaboration will operate under BOX Options Exchange, already registered as a securities exchange in the USA.

Shortly after this announcement, tZero went on to announce that a private equity firm from Hong Kong, GSR Capital, were going to purchase tZero Security Tokens to the value of $160 million, in agreement with SAFE – the Simple Agreement for Future Equity. So far, in the form of SAFEs, tZero has already raised around $168 million and all proceeds from the ongoing STO will be used for financing the BOX partnership.

Templum

Using its subsidiary company, Templum Markets LLC, the Templum platform is for two things – primary issuance of tokenized assets, and the secondary trading of those tokens. Templum has clearly decided that we need yet another acronym in the world so, rather than using the existing one of STO, they are using TAO instead – Tokenized Asset Offering.

In February of this year, Templum managed to acquire Liquid M Capital. This enabled them to access an ATS, which, in turn, enabled another market. Using the ATS, Templum is able to offer liquidity for any security that they tokenize and still remain in compliance with the security regulations. Templum has kept its head down for some time now but, in April, they hit the headlines when they managed to raise a sum of $10 million from the SBI Group in Japan. This was used for financing the trading platform development and to help with an expansion planned to go across Asia.

The platform looks as if it is live now but has few listings on it. So Far, the only company that has successfully conducted a TAO on the platform is BanQu and BCAP are the only ones to have completed a secondary trade. Like all the security token trading though, all trading will be limited to those accredited investors, assuming that the Taos have been structured so that they comply with Reg D.

Lastly, Templum and CUSIP Global Services have recently partnered to bring about a system of issuing standardized ID numbers to the security tokens. Right now, this honor will only go to those tokens that have been listed on Templum Markets, but there is scope for this to become a standard practice across the entire industry.

SharesPost

SharesPost is one of the oldest, starting out in 2009. It is the company that launched the online industry for the private equity secondaries and they now have a massive user base of more than 50,000 investors (all accredited) and have been responsible for the facilitation of over $4 billion in shares transactions for over 200 different technology companies.

SharesPost easily recognized the huge opportunity on offer by security tokens and in May they announced that a revamp of their ATS facility was in progress so that they could facilitate security token trading. In June, they also announced the closure of a $15 million Series C round, which Kenetic Capital and LUN Partner led so that they could build on their ATS further and carry out an expansion into Asia. The CEO of SharesPost says that their strategy is based on the creation of a global, unified marketplace for tokenized and traditional securities for private companies. If it all goes as they plan, the new platform should be in operation by the end of 2018.

Coinbase

The last from the USA is Coinbase. Anyone in the Cryptocurrency world knows this name and in June they announced that they were on target to start operating as a fully regulated broker-dealer. This will enable them to start secondary trading in security tokens and is huge news for the company. And, not long ago, Coinbase made the announcement that their plans were signed off on by FINRA. So, how did this all start?

The answer, as it so often is, was money. In one hit, Coinbase managed to acquire no less than three companies – Digital Wealth LLC, Venovate Marketplace Inc., and Keystone Capital Corp. The three acquisitions provided Coinbase with the licenses required to make their plans a real possibility in terms of regulatory compliance. Those licenses are the ATS license, a Broker-dealer licenses and an RIA (Registered Investment Advisor) license. It all fell into place when the deal was signed off on, very quickly, by the regulators.

Australian Securities Exchange

Leaving the USA behind we head over to Australia where the Australian Securities Exchange, one of the biggest in the world, has woken up and smelled the coffee. The ASX has an average turnover every day of more than A$4.5 billion along with an almost A$2 trillion market capitalization. The ASX is listed in the top 15 exchange groups in the world and deserves some credit for being one of the first to see what benefits DLT (Distributed Ledger Technology and tokenized shares were offering.

In 2015, the ASX were starting to explore the possible applications of DLT and, in December 2017 they announced that they were replacing their system of registry, settlement and clearing with a system based on DLT. This system was developed in a collaboration with Digital Assets, one of the largest blockchain providers of infrastructure to the major financial institutions. By doing this, the ASX gained a name for itself as one of the biggest converts to the blockchain among the major financial institutions. The rollout is targeted to happen between the fourth quarter of 2020 and the first quarter of 2021.

There is a catch though. The system will only operate on a permissioned and private blockchain; the participants must have received clearance to use the blockchain and the only party who will be able to commit the transactions onto the ledger will be ASX. What this means in simple terms, is that it will end up as a centralized network.

However, it has been pointed out that, long-term, this might not be the best move. The trend of tokenizing assets continues to grow and the decentralized networks are the ones that offer the best promise – they are the only ones that can create global financial systems that are open, unified and interoperable. Those who centralize their networks are likely to be left out in the cold.

SIX Swiss Exchange

The SIX Swiss Exchange is based in Zurich, and used to be known as the SWX Swiss Exchange; it is the main stock exchange in Switzerland and is also the largest in Europe, boasting a market cap of at least $1.7 billion. In July, SIX jumped on the security token bandwagon with an announcement that they were starting to build an infrastructure that would integrate trading, settlement and custody of tokenized securities. The project is named SIX Digital Exchange, or SDX, and it claims to be the very first in the world offering an end-to-end solution for the markets for tokenized assets. Their services will include both trading and issuance and will also tokenize securities that already exist and assets that are not bankable, as a way of creating liquidity for assets that were previously illiquid. And in time, SDX will gain the "golden seal of approval"; regulation by FINMA (the Swiss financial regulator) and backing from the Swiss National back, exactly the same as the SIX exchange has.

According to SIX, the project is going to be rolled out in stages with the first expected to go live in 2019. According to the CEO of SX, Jos Dijsselhof, this is the start of a brand new era in infrastructures for capital markets. What is happening now in the digital space is going to be the future and isn't going anywhere; all that is really left is for the gap between traditional and digital financial services and communities to be bridged by the financial industry.

London Stock Exchange

The London Stock Exchange is one of the oldest in the world and a recent announcement from them has caused no small amount of excitement among the blockchain community. It has been reported that the London Stock Exchange Group, or LSEG, together with the biggest financial regulator in the UK, the Financial Conduct Authority, have teamed up with two UK startups – 20|30 and Nivuara – to tokenize securities for a UK company, fully compliant with all the regulations. The partnership will target accredited and institutionalized investors, leveraging the LSEG Turquoise platform – this is a hybrid platform for the European equities. The tokens will be based on Ethereum so it would be reasonable to assume that they will be of the ERC20 standard.

In September, 20|30 started work as the first of the companies to start testing the process and, after a one-year lockup period, providing it all goes as it should do, the service will be launched publicly. This will allow small and mid-sized corporations and startups to start tokenizing their company shares and, perhaps unsurprisingly, the pipeline of companies waiting to join is quite large already.

Although this is not quite up to the ambitious standards of the Zurich plan, this is a huge step forward for the UK, especially as the date of them leaving the European Union draws nearer, and it is one of the most exciting of all the exchange plans to be announced.

Malta Stock Exchange

Last but by no means least, we have the Malta Stock Exchange. Recently, a collaboration was announced between Neufund and MSX, one of the innovation vehicles for MSE (Malta Stock Exchange), and a partnership with Binance. Both of these ventures are set to create a stock exchange that is decentralized, global and EU-regulated for the purpose of listing tokenized securities and trading them. The partnerships have been designed as a way of providing accredited investors with a significant amount of liquidity when they trade with Neufund equity tokens, a goal that they have been working towards for some considerable time. All three of the parties that are involved will be conducting a pilot project, including offering tokenized equity (public) on the primary market for Neufund. The aim is to have these tokens tradable on the Binance platform along with other crypto exchanges, but this will depend on approvals for listing and regulations.

Why does this matter? This deal is representing what is possibly the very first complete ecosystem, fully regulated, for the tokenization of equities, from issuance right through to trading. Malta is already well established as a blockchain community haven with some of the biggest players like OKEx and Binance relocating to what has fondly become known as #BlockchainIsland! Recent reforms in terms of regulations have proved that the country has a forward-thinking, progressive mindset and many of the legal uncertainties that surround the technology have been removed.

These are just some of the projects, the major ones, in the security token domain but, as time goes on, we expect to see more and more joining the queue. As always, care should be taken when selecting a platform to ensure you get one that is reputable and above board.

Chapter 9: The Status Quo in STOs

Right now, it is not clear how any of the existing STO platforms and the upcoming ones, will be able to address the many problems or to capitalize on the many opportunities that the STOs are set to provide the investments scene. The investment and financial markets that are based on the blockchain are still very young with many new start-ups and some of the established companies like Coinbase just dipping their toes in the securities scene.

We can get some idea of how this market can potentially grow by looking at the projects are that are just now stepping into the fray.

Issuance Platforms:

- **Polymath** – a protocol that helps facilitate the issuance of security tokens that are legally compliant and including all legal requirements for the specific security.

- **Swarm Fund** – a platform that used the SRC20 protocol for tokenization of real-world assets. The protocol is the standard int eh cryptographic world for security tokens and for listing them for sale.

- **Harbor** – an open-source platform that is used for assisting traditional investments to make the move to the blockchain, making regulatory compliance more streamlined. The platform uses private sales that are fully compliant with Reg-D.

- **Securitize** – a service that is fully compliant with the regulations and makes security tokens streamlines registration for investors in KYC and AML and all other legal requirements.

- **Jibrel Network** – a network that makes currencies, commodities, equities and other assets and instruments (financial) as ERC20 tokens on Ethereum.

Exchanges

- **Coinbase** – a well-known popular exchange for cryptocurrency has recently acquired three companies that will allow them to offer security token trading on a regulated platform.

- **tZero** – currently in traditional equities but has plans to expand into security tokens. The current tZero token is ERC20 that pays token holders 10% of the gross revenue.

- **OFN** – OpenFinance Network is an open-source platform that offers trading, clearing and settlement; a compliant security token standard has recently been created allowing for the exchange of tokens which will be issued on the blockchain.

- **Ambisafe/Orderbook** – one of the decentralized exchanges that has made investor verification an automated service, cross-referencing the requirements of the local jurisdiction with a database that contains information about token holders.

- **Bancor** – provides liquidity for tokens that connect multiple tokens to a single capital pool. Bancor is partnered with SpiCE VC whereby SpiCE VC will hold around 5% of its own capital on Banco to ensure token holders have sufficient liquidity.

- **GBX** – the Gibraltar Stock Exchange is, in its own words, "an institutional-grade token sale platform and digital asset exchange." They do say that their tokens are utility tokens but may offer security tokens at some point in the future. Currently, they list only the legally compliant, vetted tokens.

Hybrid Issuance/Exchange Platforms

- **Templum** – a platform for the issuance and trading of security tokens. Fully compliant with the regulations, Templum is also registered as an ATS and as a broker-dealer

- **Securrency** – another platform fully compliant with regulations that offer trading and transference of security tokens, as well as services such as confirmation of investor eligibility, KYC/AML, and a range of tax services.

- **Vaultbank** – a platform for stock trading that has only just launched; will be including security token issuance and crypto trading.

Aside from these, there are also some tokenized securities already in existence, including the BCAP securities, Lottery.com, Science Blockchain, SpiCE VC, PropertyCoin, 22X Fund, and others.

It is only to be hoped that the platforms can evolve or we will see others that will offer extensive and clear information, as well as business plans worth investing in, on projects that will be available for both small and large investors. This will allow anyone to get involved while, at the same time, removing the need for pre-sales or including lock-in periods that are reasonable – these will restrict investors from buying and then selling straight away.

As these platforms begin to mature and go live, the picture will get clearer as to the effect that they will potentially have on the markets for traditional securities. They could bring in a brand new way of fundraising for organizations, individuals, and for communities. Or they could just be nothing more than a tool that will stifle innovation and concentrate wealth in small areas, challenging the current status quo we see in the economic world today.

Security token offerings offer a potential method of crowdfunding, allowing communities, smaller investors, even groups to launch brand new enterprises that will result in the birth of a new sharing economy. However, it is important that we are careful not to allow the government, banks and bigger businesses to co-opt the new movement, at the same time ensuring that we also don't reject some of the more, perhaps critical aspects, of the traditional offerings we see today in terms of investment.

Chapter 10: Four Companies to Watch in 2019

In the coming months, we expect to see security tokens stepping forward and becoming the new cryptocurrency, the latest and perhaps safest digital investment method. There are some projects that are worth keeping an eye on and these are the top four.

Polymath

The Polymath platform uses the ST20 standard to ensure the security tokens are fully compliant with governmental regulations for the issuance of digital securities. The Polymath platform is similar to Ethereum but, rather than the utility tokens that ICO platforms create, Polymath offers equity in different companies. This model already has a regulatory framework that is fully established. Polymath focuses its efforts on AML, KYC and other legalities ensuring that the securities laws are fully complied with, much of this because ICOs have come under close scrutiny from governmental regulators in the last two years.

An ICO and an STO have one major difference – the equity stake in a given company. Some of the best examples of the difficulties that the early projects on the blockchain faced were the legal issues that surround Tezos, a cryptocurrency created by Arthur Breitman, a Morgan Stanley Analyst, and the efforts of Ripple to get separation from the XRP token. It is worth bearing in mind that most of the networks, the foundations, even the tokens, are interchangeable with very blurry lines between them.

When the ICO concept was finally proven, so many jumped onto the bandwagon and it grew to a huge business. In 2017, over $5.5 billion was raised by ICOs and in 2018, this had more than doubled to more than $13 billion. However, this kind of money always attracts the baddies and more than $100 million was lost because of ICO exit scams.

Polymath says they have the answer, and this has sparked off the rise of interest in STOs, with Polymath developing and building one of the most solid ecosystems based on the blockchain. But does this mean the end of the ICO?

Before we can answer that, we need to look at the POLY token and how it is performing on the crypto market.

The POLY Token

The supply of the POLY token in circulation is almost 300,000,000 out of a finite supply of 1,000,000,000. The highest price we have seen to date is $1.59 in February; right now, the price is just over $0.15, but it is steadily rising again, and it mustn't be forgotten – Bitcoin started out at a really low price and look what happened there!

Polymath was responsible for creating the ST20 standard, but they use POLY as a stake. POLY is an ERC20 token that comes from the Ethereum blockchain and this means that although Polymath does enable security tokens, the native token is a utility.

The Polymath ICO was the very first one registered with the SEC and is fully compliant. A private token sale raised more than $59 million, with only accredited investors allowed into the sale and, once it got going, it went on to pave the way for all other cryptocurrencies to follow.

Polymath had an initial supply of 240,000,000 and this was airdropped to all participants who had registered interest in the sale by January 10, 2018. The founding team retained the rest and it is worth noting that you cannot mine POLY. In the same way that Eth fuels Ethereum transactions, so POLY fuels Polymath transactions.

Every day, trades amounting to $4 million in POLY are carried out and a number of cryptocurrency exchanges provide support, including Upbit, CoinZest, Bittrex, Binance, LATOKEN and Huobi. Some of the trading pairs include POLY/ETH, POLY/BTC, and some fiat currencies such as POLY/KRW.

Because POLY is an ERC20 utility token, all wallets compatible with the ERC20 standard will support it, including MyEtherWallet and the Ledger range of hardware wallets.

Harbor

The next company to keep an eye on is Harbor, a compliance protocol that is fully decentralized and designed as a global standard for the issuance and trade of securities on the blockchain. The people behind the platform are David Sacks, Aris Amano and Bob Remeika, and they all have a common goal – to redefine the issuance and trade of crypto securities on the blockchain.

The idea came to them when they were attempting to raise money through an ICO but were faced with many challenges – both compliance and technical. When they looked further into it, the team found that many companies wanted their assets tokenized but were stymied by the regulations and all the technical requirements that went with it.

The way Harbor operates is quite simple – the process of tokenization is simplified to make the compliance process easier and more transparent. To do this, they formed a regulated token which is called R-Token and this is an ERC20 token. However, it has extra coding which is designed to make it easy to check the on-chain whitelist, which is the regulator service.

This whitelist also has other roles – it can certify some of the assets, it can set the requirements for KYC, AML and for investor accreditation. For example, when a real estate sale is made under FIRPTA – Foreign Investment in Real Property Tax Act – the tax must be withheld when the investors are foreigners to the country.

The R-Token involves four main steps:

1. An investor orders a certain amount of a preferred R-Token

2. The chosen R-Token will follow the relevant regulator service that monitors and ensures legal compliance

3. If the investor doesn't meet the requirements, an error is returned and the transfer will not take place

4. If an investor meets the requirements, the transfer of the R-Token will complete and will be confirmed

The R-Token is an open source protocol on the blockchain. Long-term, the goal is for smart contracts to be published for the R-Tokens and for the regulator service to bring in a standardized method of issuing and exchanging tokenized securities. The other features of an R-Token are:

- The R-Token is ERC20 compatible

- Transfers can only happen between individuals that are compliant or whitelisted

- It has a flexible framework that allows for securities regulations, such as AML and KYC, to be enforced

- Regulation compliance is built-in at token level on all trading platforms.

Harbor has one primary aim – to assist companies in issuing tokens that are fully compliant – an aim that is set to become a real game changer for those involved in the blockchain.

The blockchain industry is very much aware and appreciative of the fact that a lack of regulation can attract harsh regulation, but the use of R-Token and other verified protocols means that tokens can be issued by any company, using laws that already exist, to raise the money they need quite easily.

Securitize

Securitize is one of the latest offerings on the Blockchain and it offers complete, end-to-end support for anyone looking to tokenize assets. The Securitize platform is very flexible and offers a backend that is impressive, helping to manage investors when tokens are issued.

The platform has garnered a great deal of support from the community because of the unique features it offers and the fact that tokenization takes place inside of the existing framework. It is for this reason that many exchanges like Blocktrade and SharesPost, and lots of companies have gone into a partnership with the platform.

Most notably, Securitize can integrate with third-party apps operating on the Ethereum blockchain, the implication being that individual companies will be able to develop their clients, choose which interface they want and, if they need to, they can work with third-party developers.

The development team behind Securitize are committed to enhancing security on the platform and this has led to the way that assets, capital and funds are managed for investors to be redefined. This approach has also led to an increase in the chance of Securitize becoming, if not the top, one of the best of the STO platforms available today.

At the start of December, Science Blockchain announced that they will be working with Securitize to help upgrade their SCI security token to make compliance easier. Right now the SCI tokens in circulation are frozen while the move is made from TokenHub to Securitize and all holders who also have other tokens on TokenHub will be kept informed of the process.

Templum

The final company to watch in 2019 is Templum, a platform that seeks to offer initial security token sales and an exchange for trading. There are pros and cons to the Templum platform:

- Because it has gone into an early partnership with Indiegogo, a popular brand name, Templum has easily gained an STO with a brand name; Aspen Digital Security Token, the first branded STO to be owned by one of the Fortune 500's.

- Templum could have quite an unfair advantage in access to institutional funds because previous experiences have provided them with a very deep family office network.

- It is an ambitious project to launch a platform that is both for issuance and secondary trading of security tokens. If Templum launches successfully, it will be the only platform to offer both.

- The timeline for launching the secondary trading venue is not very clear.

Assuming that the information on LinkedIn regarding the employees is correct, it would appear that Templum has few technical developers compared to its nearest competitors like tZero. tZero has 15 technical developers, representing 30% of their company while Templum has just 4, representing 22% of their company, quite a significant difference.

There is also fierce competition from crypto exchanges already in existence, along with the smaller stock exchanges and this is a big threat to the likes of Templum as they could take what early liquidity there is for the security tokens. This could force Templum into launching into an environment that is highly competitive and not altogether favorable.

Their Vision

Templum has a vision and that is to facilitate the expansion and growth of tokenized securities and that is going to be done by the implementation of best practices and standards for security token offerings and secondary trading.

Their team is made up of 18 people, four of which are technical which means that 22% of the company is in charge of the technical development for the platform and venue. Some of their experience is made up as follows:

- CEO Christopher Pallotta. Selection Committee member and Director Associative of the MIT E14 fund since 2014. In 2015 he took the post of MD for Raptor Capital Management and in 2017 he became one of the co-founders of Templum.

- COO Joseph K Latone Jr. Worked for Intercapital Securities LLC, an investment advisor and registered broker-dealer with FINRA. He was also the President of COO for another FINRA registered broker-dealer, Ouisa Capital LLC.

Because the initial STOs are technically challenging, not to mention the compliance challenges, and because they have no secondary market liquidity, the tokens tend to lose quite a bit of their advantage against the traditional private equities. Templum aims to solve this problem by offering a portal for primary offerings with full support for regulatory compliance as well as offering the ATS for secondary trading. At the moment, there is no evidence of any trading activity.

Conclusion

Thank you for taking the time to read my guide; I hope that it has been of help to you. You should now understand more about security tokens and STOs, how they differ from ICOs and other similar projects.

Security tokens are the future of blockchain technology. While Bitcoin and other cryptocurrencies kick started the craze, everything must come to an end sooner or later or be surpassed by other technologies and that's what is happening here. Bitcoin will continue to exist, Ethereum and its smart contracts will carry on, but security tokens will take the number one spot as Blockchain technology arises as the real disruptive force.

While the thrill of Bitcoin was in the fact that it was unregulated, for many investors, regulation is important as it gives them some guarantee over the safety of their money and what they are investing in. Financial services have been involved in one way or another in blockchain technology for some time and the regulatory bodies have been champing at the bit to get their hands on it.

With security tokens you get the best of both worlds; you get the security and you get the chance to own a bit of something that would normally be out of your price range. Don't hesitate, get in on the action today and watch the market go!

Thank you once again for reading my guide.

Bonus Chapter 1: 7 Predictions on the Future of STOs

When Bitcoin and other subsequent cryptocurrencies, followed by the ICOs entered the market, predictions on their future and their performance were everywhere. The same thing is happening with the security token offerings and these are seven of the hottest predictions for 2019 and the coming years:

1. STOs will overtake ICOs in funds raised by 2020.

We have already discussed that some experts claim STOs will soon overtake ICOs. The first prediction hence doesn't come as a surprise. Many related articles have been published by industry insiders and entrepreneurs in the last months, including on outlets like medium.com and bitcoinist.com. The reasons for this are of course primarily the additional certainty that comes from having regulator-approved token generation events, but also that the "ICO party has come to an end" as a commentator put it in a related article on Bitcoinist.

Of course, the scene is still too much in its infancy for us to predict how quickly this is going to happen. But with a rapid rise in the demand and popularity of STOs and the growing skepticism and fading excitement about "yet another utility token and ICO", it is not far-fetched to predict STOs overtaking ICOs in 2020. For 2019 in turn we expect to see a rapid increase in STOs being marketed and discussed as well as a general consensus arising that security tokens are superior to and offer more common use cases than classical utility tokens.

2. IPOs will soon be left by the wayside as STOs become a far more attractive alternative.

Okay, I will admit that this is a bit of a stretch. But I am absolutely convinced that STOs will come to be seen as potentially the best alternative to a classical IPO, especially when the funds to be raised are in the double-digit million range. Yes, there are still many hesitant and skeptical observers on the sidelines, but let me tell you: they are watching!

From discussions with industry members and start-ups at events and meet-ups, I have heard time and time again that people are hoping that STOs will finally become a valid and legally approved option. Clearly the demand is there. And it only makes sense that many parties don't want to be the very first as there are still some legal challenges and risks out there. But once the first successful STOs have come about in their country or target markets, the courage will increase and the number of STOs to be held rise dramatically.

Sure, IPOs will still and always be there. But STOs will eventually end up at eye level with IPOs and certainly be the better option in many cases.

3. We will see more jurisdictions passing relevant laws on how STOs should be conducted – an important point to check because the laws will likely differ from jurisdiction to jurisdiction.

While I wouldn't dare to predict if this will already be the case for 2019, it will come in early 2020 at the latest. More and more regulators in jurisdictions around the world are looking into and examining various use cases early STO movers have filed. I personally have helped 4 companies get their documents and white papers together in order to file a request with the regulators in their countries (EU-based).

Currently of course all filed STOs are examined on a case-by-case basis. This is burdensome and lengthy. The more requests and filings come in by start-ups wanting to hold STOs, the stronger the pressure on regulators will get. Yes, even regulators can face some pressure and will have to adjust accordingly. The first STOs approved and held in these jurisdictions with the regulators evaluations and decisions will provide guidelines and fundamentals on the basis of which – eventually – laws and rules will be passed that all STOs have to obey.

By 2020 probably, some countries will have a framework in place so regulators no longer have to conduct burdensome audits on all cases filed. Start-ups will be better able to prepare their financial models to be compliant with these regulations. Which countries will be the first to pass such laws? Aside from Malta, my bet is on Switzerland, Liechtenstein and Singapore.

As these laws are passed, attention has to be paid to the way in which they are going to differ. Some differences are bound to be there as countries compete in attracting STOs to their country.

4. **There will be a standardization of the security tokens and their connected rights.**

As discussed earlier, currently there are vast differences in the rights that go with proposed security tokens. While this variety is perfectly normal for a newly evolving field, it represents a major obstacle to the widescale adoption of STOs as a new form of raising funds.

With more and more regulators working on regulation and laws surrounding STOs (or drafting them), it is more likely that certain use cases will come to dominate over others. Maybe it will be regulators allowing certain rights but putting restrictions on others. Most likely, certain security tokens will be allowed in some jurisdictions but not in others – going back to the competition between various jurisdictions for a newly evolving and attractive fundraising method.

While variety might exist between the jurisdictions, for each jurisdiction itself – at least this is my prediction – the regulations will likely favor certain rights over others, or outright forbid certain security tokens currently proposed.

5. **While there will be plenty of use cases for security tokens, the most common one, at least to start with, will be automation of profit share and dividend payments.**

This goes along with many things previously stated. Most importantly however, it is my conversations with start-ups, founders and observers at start-up events and meet-ups that causes me to make this prediction. Token economics are in discussion. But what the markets are really craving are cheaper, more efficient and legally compliant fundraising methods. STOs are to the best of my knowledge the perfect and best candidate to fill this need.

Once regulations are in place, there will be a run for them. Yes, anything is possible, and the markets are hard to predict. But the demand is clearly there and eventually it will pave itself a way – one way or another.

6. Eventually, most of the companies who conduct an STO will have no participation in any blockchain project.

This may seem paradoxical or weird at first, but it only makes sense if prediction 5 comes true. Look, right now we are all about ICOs, Blockchain and Token Economics. We only see business models that utilize the blockchain and create some sort of token economy in which users and clients exchange tokens for their services. We are still in a utility token-dominated cryptosphere.

But many if not most of the companies conducting STOs to raise funds simply want to do so because it is cheaper and more efficient than the lengthy and burdensome process of an IPO. The majority of companies conducting STOs will only use the blockchain – or more importantly – blockchain-based smart contracts – to issue their tokens, make them tradable on the secondary market and automatically pay profit share or conduct votings (depending on the token-connected rights that will prevail in coming legislation).

7. As the laws come into effect and security tokens begin to grow, we can expect competition between jurisdictions to become the most attractive location for the STO.

Take my word for it. Right now, we might see regulators as the brake pad on the STO train that wants to take off at high speed. Eventually, like pioneers in Malta, Switzerland and Liechtenstein have already realized, STOs will also come to mean business for countries and governments. Once this realization has come upon politicians in these countries, a worldwide competition will come to be.

Personally, I believe that the classical first movers in the financial markets will win the race. The European Union and the United States will probably be amongst the later-moving jurisdictions. Naturally, there are some issues as to what jurisdiction an STO is held in and where the owners of the tokens are based.

This however is beyond the scope of this book as well as my legal competence and insight and will certainly be dealt with by more competent and the responsible decision-makers in the various bodies of government and institutions.

Bonus Chapter 2: 10 STOs (& STO Companies) to Watch in 2019

Right now, there are already a few STOs doing the rounds but with the steady change in interest towards the STO and away from the ICO and the IPO, we can expect to see quite a few more appearing in 2019. Here's 10 that you should keep an eye on:

1. **Mobu** – A security token issuance protocol and a licensed exchange for security tokens

Mobu caught my attention early on and might still be my most favorite STO project of all. The South Africa-based team around Brian Golding and Juan Engelbrecht is working on a platform that will support the issuing of security tokens and offer a licensed exchange at the same time. The company describes itself as an "end-to-end solution for launching compliant security tokens". Similar to the ERC-20 standard for utility tokens, MOBU has developed the MOB20 protocol that defines a set of commands recommended for a compliant security token. According to the company, tokens using the MOB20 protocol are compliant with Reg S, Reg D and Reg A+. Moreover, the platform wants to implement a rating system for the given service providers to offer more transparency and fair pricing for investors.

Personally I have enjoyed the company's whitepaper as a very professional and structured one. The team members have a great track record, some reputable partners are also on board. What I love most though is that the company is working on solving the major pain point of different regulations for securities in different jurisdictions and trying to bring standardization to the field.

You can learn all about the project at https://mobu.io

2. **DESICO** – A completely legal and decentralized security ICO platform

Another interesting STO to watch in 2019 is the Lithuanian-based company DESICO. Similar to Mobu, it intends to create a platform on which security tokens can be issued but also traded on a securities exchange integrated into the platform. Particularly interesting is the fact, that Lithuania as an EU-country could be an important actor in the discussion and formulation of EU-specific laws for security tokens.

While the direct supervisory regulator is the Bank of Lithuania, this regulator itself has to check for compliance with all applicable EU-laws. If you are a EU-citizen, then DESICO should be particularly high on your watchlist. While the tokensale is ending on 25th of January 2019, my guess is that the token will also be in good demand thereafter.
The security token is configured in such a way that token holders receive a revenue share of 12.5% for a period of 30 years with payouts occurring every quarter.

3. **Cryptune** – A top-notch next-generation point-of-sale technology that is blockchain enabled

As the title says, Cryptune has developed a point-of-sale-software that is superior to many modern-day solutions that cause high transaction and administrative costs. Moreover, Cryptune offers a mobile wallet with which CPT users can earn reward and loyalty points. The company is based in the US and also wants to enter this market first.

The reason I personally like this STO is because of its team as well as the token structure. The founders Ricardo Cuesta and Jose Callado have long experience in retail, just as their reputable advisors have. 5% of the companies net revenue will go to investors, paid out in the form of an annual dividend. Important note: although the team is US-based, US residents are not eligible for investing unfortunately.

For more information, be sure to check https://cryptune.io

4. **BlockEstate** – A real estate fund that has been tokenized and based in the USA

The team of BlockEstate has partnered up with Polymath and CoinList's ComplyAPI in order to enable a tokenized real estate fund through which investors from around the world can invest into the US real estate market. The company lays out in its whitepaper that they are going to make use of predictive analytics and big data to identify the most profitable market sectors and then invest there.

The reason I am listing this venture as one of the top 10 to watch is that they have gathered an impressive list of advisors and will have an interesting stablecoin backed by US-American real estate. Moreover, their token economics are based on the "buyback and burn" approach. Generated profits will be leveraged to buy back tokens from token holders and subsequently destroy those tokens leading to increased token value for remaining holders and profits for those selling their tokens.

Learn more by visiting their site at https://blockestate.com

5. **Rise** – algorithmic trading technology using artificial intelligence and machine learning.

This Germany-based company is developing powerful AI-based trading algorithms that promise to make the RSE token holders solid profits. Again, it is primarily a professional whitepaper with an experienced team and well-connected advisors that has won over my trust. Moreover, we have known for some time that AI-based algorithms will surely take over the trading scene.

While the revenue model is a tad to complex for my personal taste, you might find it particularly interesting. The basic profit for token holders will come from a subordinated profit participation in the revenue generated by Rise's algorithms. Moreover, as the company licenses its technology to banks and hedge funds, 20% of these license fees will also be paid out to token holders. More complex is the option of RSE holders to use RSE tokens in their wallet as a collateral for lending capital to invest in crypto-funds.

Visit https://rise.eco to learn more about the company and its STO.

6. **Uncloak** – cyber threat detection service using the EOS Blockchain

Uncloak is based in Estonia and wants to tackle the omnipresent security threat online. It is all about a proprietary AI-based threat detection database that will be managed and filled by company-approved "hunters" and "validators". These actors will be rewarded with the platform's internal EOS UCC token whereas a classical ERC-20 token will be used for external trading. Users of the platform will have their networks checked for the identified threats.

These tokens can be converted one against the other. You can buy ERC-20 tokens and have them converted to UCC tokens to utilize the platform's threat detection services. Hunters and validators can transfer their UCC tokens into ERC-20 tokens to trade them on exchanges in case they want to liquidate their tokens. An impressive team of security industry veterans and senior advisors makes me believe this project will come to fruition.

Unfortunately the STO has been delayed a few times. Be sure to check https://uncloak.io to know when it will actually be held.

7. **hypd** – A global security token and an ambassador app

Hypd is a marketing software that allows influencers and brand owners to setup an ambassador program with individualized reward and incentive structures. Utilizing the platform's software, brand owners can define actions that if executed by fans will reward them with points that can exclusively be redeemed for brand-related prices and rewards.

While you may not be the kind of person who gets deeply engaged in such ambassador programs (I'm not), we all know how widespread the phenomenon of influencers in the social media age has become. Especially millennials between 18-29 are very active users of such program. This is why I find this project highly interesting, particularly because the target group is also in the age range most likely to be open to using tokens and wallets.

Ownership of the security token entitles to a regular dividend payment. Learn more by visiting https://hypd.co

8. **Sports Ledger** – a sports data analytics platform using smart contracts and Blockchain for tamper-proof storing of biometric data

Sports is a triple-digit billion-dollar industry. If you are anything like me, you also love to watch a good sports game and cheer for your favorite team – whatever your favorite type of sports may be. It wasn't until my younger brother started studying sport science that I realized how analytical and data-driven professional sports is these days.

Sports Ledger is being developed with exactly this target market in mind. Sporting data on a granular basis from 2005-2018 is gathered, allowing to track individual athletes in real time. Users of Sports Ledger have to buy platform tokens and can then access predictive models that analyze and try to forecast athlete's development and performance. Specific biometric tech is to be worn by athletes to feed data directly into Sports Ledger platform. Platform-internal tokens can be earned through sharing data and also be redeemed in advertising on the platform.

The company will hold its STO in Liechtenstein and has attracted an impressive team of advisors that includes some of the most sought-after blockchain experts. Date of the STO has already been postponed once, so be sure to check https://sportsledger.io for up-to-date details.

9. **Leaseum Partners** – A Security token backed by real estate that pays out dividends to investors

This one is probably the most important real estate STO I have come across. You don't just get to invest into any real estate. The company wants to set up a 250 million USD-heavy fund that invests into commercial property in New York City.

The team is made up of industry veterans and a comprehensive team of advisors that handle legal and investor relations aspects. Ownership of the security token is connected with equity ownership and entitles to a quarterly-paid dividend. If you want to find out more, go to https://leaseumpartners.com

10. **Property Coin** – Backed by Aperture this is a security token backed 100% by real estate.

References

https://icobench.com/

https://blockgeeks.com

https://coinsutra.com

https://tokeny.com

https://stocheck.com/blog

https://beyondblocks.com

https://thetokenist.io

https://medium.com

https://blog.neufund.org

https://www.ccn.com

https://cryptobriefing.com

https://www.securitize.io

About the Author

Alex Anderson is an International Business graduate and holds degrees from Carlson School of Management (Minneapolis), University of Hagen (Germany) and Vienna University of Economics and Business (Austria).

More importantly, he is a technical writer who has been writing about Blockchain technology and start-ups since June 2013. Aside from investing in numerous ICOs, he has written 12 ICO Whitepapers and 6 STO Whitepapers to date.

Alex helps Blockchain and Crypto-companies create well-researched thought leadership content for their content marketing and PR strategy.

Made in the USA
Middletown, DE
13 May 2019